Europe

Heather DiLorenzo Williams and Warren Rylands

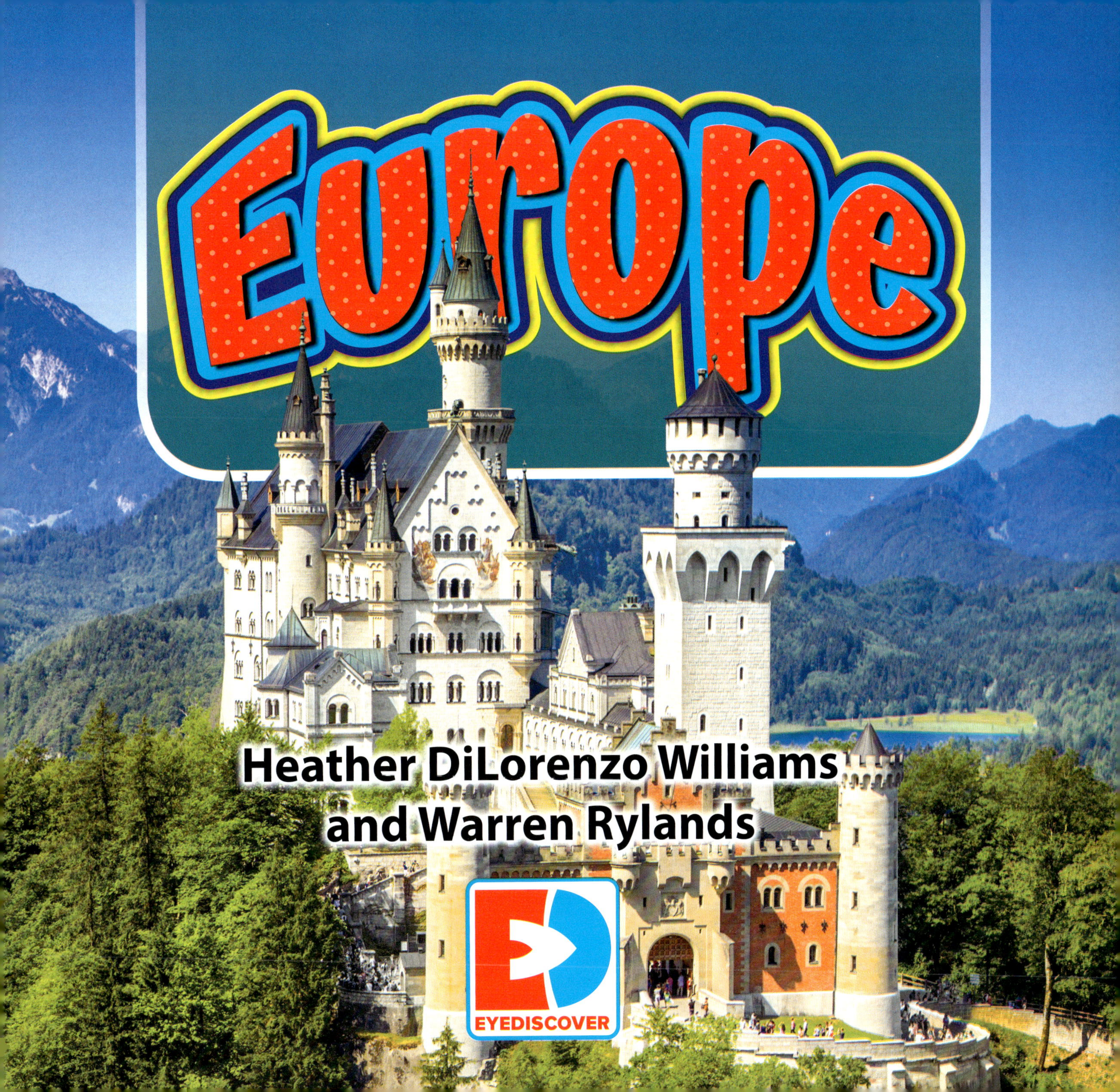

Go to **www.eyediscover.com** and enter this book's unique code.

BOOK CODE

AVG87783

EYEDISCOVER brings you optic readalongs that support active learning.

Published by AV² by Weigl
350 5th Avenue, 59th Floor New York, NY 10118
Website: www.eyediscover.com

Library of Congress Control Number: 2018953511

ISBN 978-1-4896-8329-8 (hardcover)

Printed in the United States of America
in Brainerd, Minnesota
1 2 3 4 5 6 7 8 9 0 22 21 20 19 18

082018
120917

Project Coordinator: John Willis
Designer: Mandy Christiansen

Weigl acknowledges Alamy, iStock, and Shutterstock as the primary image suppliers for this title.

EYEDISCOVER provides enriched content, optimized for tablet use, that supplements and complements this book. EYEDISCOVER books strive to create inspired learning and engage young minds in a total learning experience.

Watch
Video content brings each page to life.

Browse
Thumbnails make navigation simple.

Read
Follow along with text on the screen.

Listen
Hear each page read aloud.

Your EYEDISCOVER Optic Readalongs come alive with...

Audio
Listen to the entire book read aloud.

Video
High resolution videos turn each spread into an optic readalong.

OPTIMIZED FOR

- ☑ TABLETS
- ☑ WHITEBOARDS
- ☑ COMPUTERS
- ☑ AND MUCH MORE!

Europe

In this book, you will learn about

- where it is
- who lives there
- what animals it has

and much more!

Europe is the second-smallest continent. Only Australia is smaller than Europe.

5

Today, there are 50 countries in Europe. More people live in Russia than any other European country.

8

Great Britain is Europe's largest island. England, Scotland, and Wales are all found in Great Britain.

The smallest country in the world is Europe's Vatican City. Only about 800 people live there.

12

Moscow, Russia, is the largest city in Europe. More than 12 million people live in Moscow.

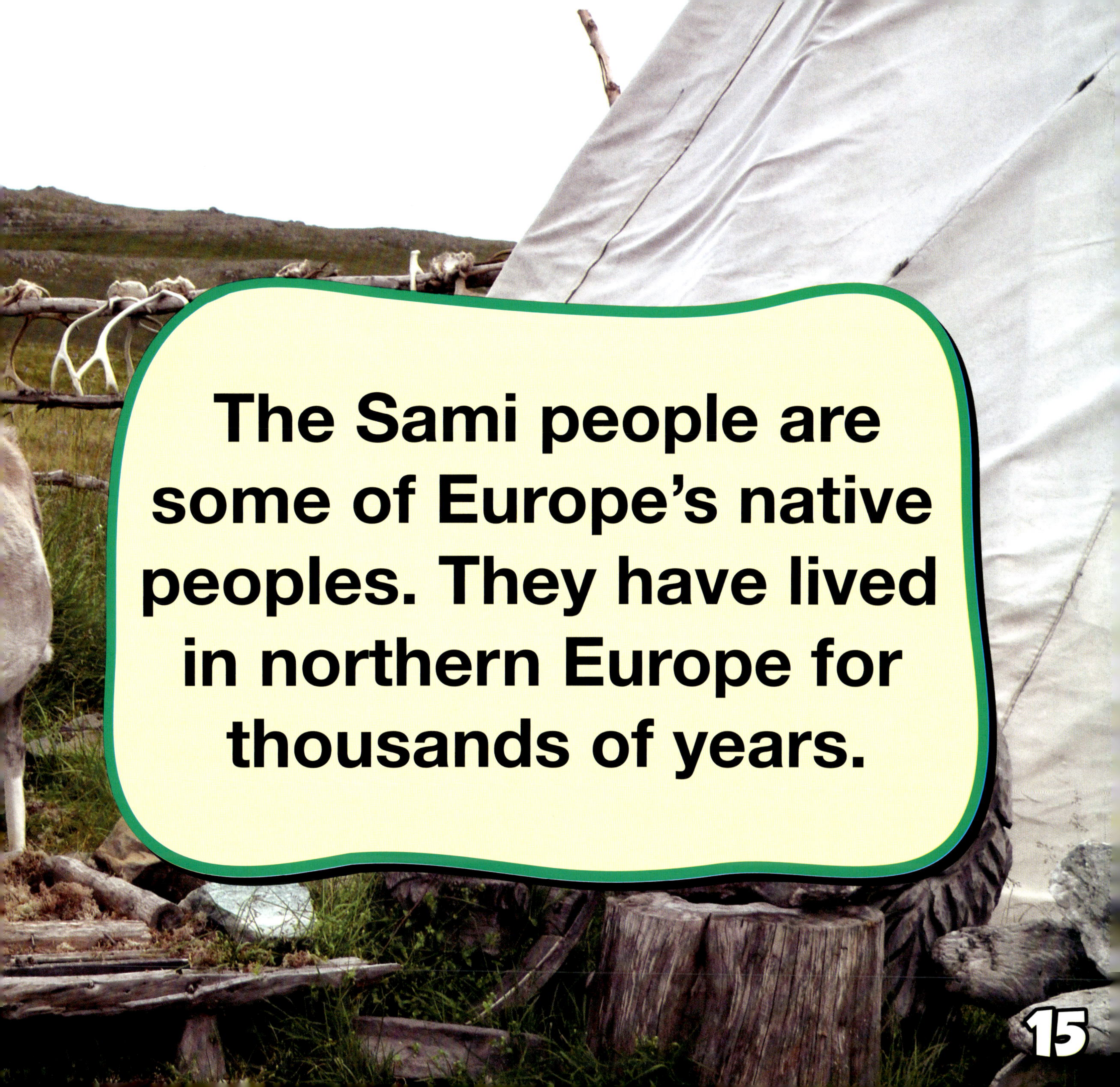

The Sami people are some of Europe's native peoples. They have lived in northern Europe for thousands of years.

Europe is also home to many different animals. These include foxes, wild boar, and bats.

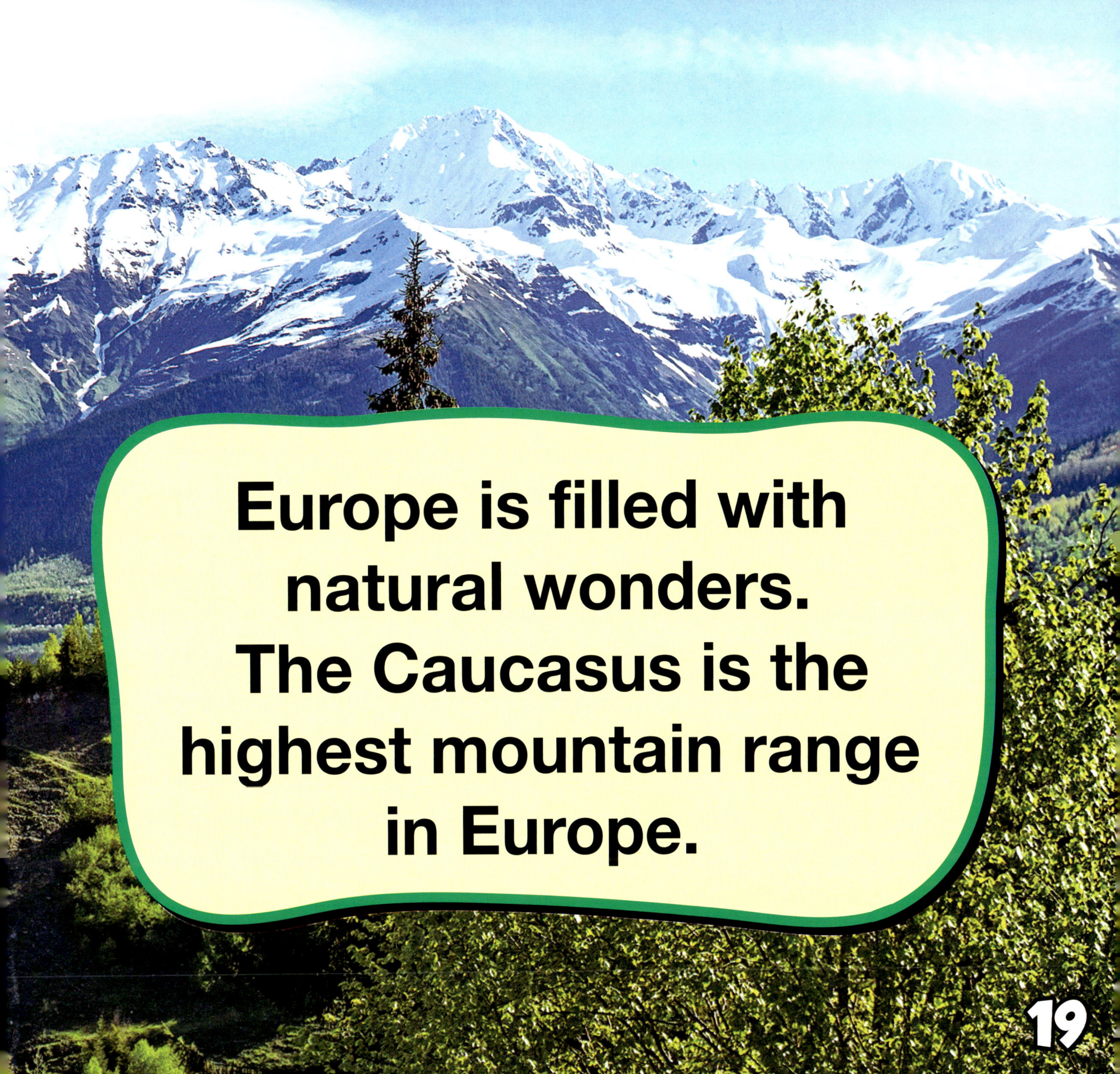

Europe is filled with natural wonders. The Caucasus is the highest mountain range in Europe.

Europe is a beautiful continent. It is home to many different people, languages, and cultures.

With **89 million** tourists each year, **France** is the most visited country in the world.

Stonehenge, an ancient man-made stone circle in **England**, is more than **5,000** years old.

Mount Elbrus is Europe's tallest mountain. It is **18,510** feet tall. (5,642 meters)

There are **26** **official languages** spoken in **Europe.**

More than **740 million** people live in **Europe** today.

Russia is the largest country in the world. It is part of both Europe and Asia.

KEY WORDS

Research has shown that as much as 65 percent of all written material published in English is made up of 300 words. These 300 words cannot be taught using pictures or learned by sounding them out. They must be recognized by sight. This book contains 37 common sight words to help young readers improve their reading fluency and comprehension. This book also teaches young readers several important content words, such as proper nouns. These words are paired with pictures to aid in learning and improve understanding.

Page	Sight Words First Appearance
4	is, only, second, than, the
6	any, are, country, in, live, more, other, people, there
9	all, and, found, great
10	about, city, world
15	for, have, of, some, they, years
16	also, animals, different, home, many, these, to
19	with
20	a, it

Page	Content Words First Appearance
4	Australia, continent, Europe
6	countries, European, Russia
9	England, Great Britain, Scotland, Wales
10	Vatican City
13	Moscow
15	native, northern, Sami
16	bats, foxes, wild boar
19	Caucasus, mountain
20	cultures, languages

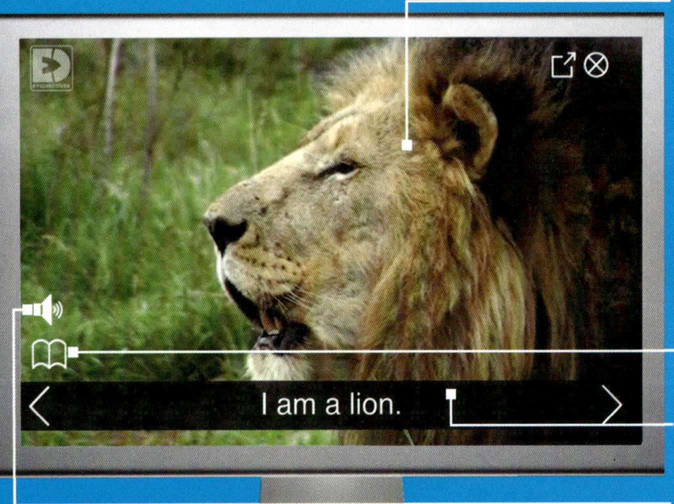

Watch
Video content brings each page to life.

Browse
Thumbnails make navigation simple.

Read
Follow along with text on the screen.

Listen
Hear each page read aloud.

Go to www.eyediscover.com and enter this book's unique code.

BOOK CODE

AVG87783